The Jelley Cupboard

THE JELLEY CUPBOARD

Poems About Life, Death, and Other Sticky Stuff

By Dawn Jelley

The Jelley Cupboard

Poems About Life, Death, and Other Sticky Stuff

Copyright © 2007 Dawn Jelley
ISBN 978-1-4303-2698-4
Printed in USA

First paperback edition September 2007
Published by: Lulu.com
Cover illustration and cover design: Eric Downer

For Eric --

my cover artist, my confidant, my love, and my friend.

Contents

Introduction

I am sure many people can give other poets credit for inspiring them and I am no exception. However my story of inspiration is rather in reverse. While working as a hospice nurse manager I was involved in our weekly interdisciplinary team meetings. We always started the meeting with centering, which involved on some occasions inspiration in the form of poetry. It was on that day our medical director recited from heart a poem about death through a hungry bear in autumn. I had no idea who had written the poem or that the poet was famous but instantly felt if anyone could write poetry about death then surely I could as well. After all I had spent the last 12 years working every day with death, assisting people on their journeys, whether it be a welcome relief from suffering or a tumultuous slide kicking and screaming into the beyond.

Within a week I had completed two poems about death. It was as if all those years of witness and sharing were waiting to bubble up and spill out, in black and white with pen and paper. "I Am Not Ready" and "Stolen" were written. Interestingly they were both about the unfairness of death. "I am not ready" speaking from the position of a young soul who knew he was dying but felt he was just not ready. The majority of the population does not spend every day with death; in fact they spend most of their days avoiding the taboo subject. One of the lessons I learned from my job is the importance of living every day, doing the things you want to do, saying the things you should say to the people you should say them to. I find it hard to think of anyone being glad to die young but I feel if at least you had lived every day to its fullest then you are more prepared than most.

I wrote "Stolen" for all my patients who I felt had been tortured by their illness, everyday fighting to readjust to how their body was changing, slowly not all at once, but in torturous increments. Their beauty, dignity and independence all taken cell by cell. Often dying people get angry at their loved ones, and many times it is because they are losing control of their life, so they often hold on even tighter. "Stolen" speaks of this loss.

I have been lucky to be healthy in my lifetime and so have never had to face death first hand, however I attempt to write many of the poems as if I were in the shoes of my patients and families. As I wrote more poetry I was inspired by a book I read that warned me not to die with my music still inside of me. I believe one form of my music is my poetry. I am hopeful that the stories and lives I have been witness to, once written down and shared will help others with their journeys and may then offer some strength.

So as I neared my fortieth birthday and I was now up to fifty-three poems the next obvious step would be to publish them. With the help of my family, the struggles and successes of my patients and their families were now on the verge of being bound.

However the poems I wrote were not only for my patients and their families but I also found them personally healing. Writing these poems helped me to process and to validate my emotions in caring for the dying. I found like turning on a tap, once they began to flow, out poured poem after poem. I started with the poems about death but it wasn't long before I dabbled into other topics such as traveling, relationships, and the whimsical. The remainder of my poems fell into the last chapter, which I call the Sticky Stuff. The sticky stuff for me is about the things that I would like to keep in my cupboard, away from prying eyes, but if we all share our sticky stuff, perhaps it isn't quite so sticky after all, or perhaps others will learn and not get quite as sticky as me. The poems are not just about the tough days, but the inspiration to get through them, live through them and move forward.

When a door closes you have a choice to stay there or move in the direction that is destined for you, guided by your faith, supported by your family, inspired by those that have trodden before. As I walk on I listen to my mantra "focus on those things you can change and not on those you cannot". It is easy to get distracted, spend energy in futility even if by passion. So rest a while on your journey and read some poems in the first chapter on the biggest thing you cannot change and that is death. But lets begin with my tribute to the poet that initially inspired me.

Meeting Mary

I met her first as a stranger, through her poem
read out loud by a colleague,
speaking of death through
a hungry bear in autumn.
I declared that if a famous poet can write on death,
so can I.
So I began.

It was a modest door I opened
yet words tumbled down like tears onto my paper.
Years of witness to what death brings
brought up from the depths of within,
almost from a sobbing ache.
Years pushed down and packed down
away from sight,
at once let free to sing as the kettle comes to boil.

I met her next as a poet,
reading from her work
to a crowd captured into a standing ovation by

their connection to her words.

I had waited to see how she wore the pain
of forty years of love now lost,
and how far she had trod the path to healing.
She then appeared before me,
unkempt with tousled hair,
as if she were the woods and the wildlife
she speaks of in her poems.

She had spoken to the crowd
with unassuming passion
of the call of the earth,
the spirit and the journey.
She spoke to me of the rescued seagull in her bathtub.

Death

Okay, so the title of the book is Life, Death and Other Sticky Stuff, and yet my first chapter is Death. "Shouldn't it be Life?", I hear you say. Well I thought the Life chapter would be a nice sandwich between Death and the poems about sticky stuff. So here we are starting with the chapter Death.

Death can intrigue us and at the same time like a porcupine's quills can scare us away. Many people choose to wait until death comes to them before they face it, but for me I chose a career that surrounded me by death everyday. I began my work with Hospice and directly with death 14 years ago. I wasn't scared of working with dying, in fact I felt it was a privilege and of all the nursing I have done could see so clearly the difference I was making in people's lives. From helping to control their pain, to feeling comfortable asking someone if they were afraid to die, and also not being afraid to reply when someone asked me what could they expect during their death. My work helped me question my mortality on a daily basis and even though I still don't have the answers to life and death, after all my work I am much more at ease with my own mortality.

I began my nurse training when I was 18 years old, and emerged three and a half years later into a world of medicine where increasingly people believed they could fix every illness and complaint. Doctors would find it difficult to say that there was not any more treatment and that their time was running out, yet many of my patients needed this time to prepare for their death. I remember very clearly speaking to one lady after her husband's death. She said every week he looked thinner and worse, but is doctor kept saying how well he was doing and kept up the treatment. A week later he died and they were both totally unprepared. She said she had wished the doctor had been more honest and regretted the time she had lost.

After nursing school, some of my friends moved on to more training and to become midwives, my career lead me to become a midwife of death. As surely as you need assistance coming into this world, then it makes sense that you would need assistance in leaving. Especially knowing the vast baggage of unfinished business many people leave until the end. So for the last thirteen years I have been involved in the delicate balance of helping people die in the manner of their choice. That might sound like a funny thing to say but I think one of the hardest parts of working with death is allowing people to die in their own way. I find that many people die how they have lived. If they have lived a life of chaos and turmoil, then often the journey to their death can follow a similar course. I remember one day, I visited a house that had classical music playing, with candles burning and a gentle atmosphere. The next house I visited, the gentleman was also bed bound and intermittently conscious and yet the TV blared and there were children jumping around his hospital bed playing with his bed controls. The first instinct might be to turn on the classical music and light candles but that's the way that I would want to die, not him. He died the way he lived. It was comforting to him and the only way he knew.

That situation was easy though compared to the choices that some people make, which may not be in a physical chaos but to die in spiritual or emotional pain. I looked after a gentleman who chose not to take his medication because he felt he deserved his cancer pain. He had spent years as an alcoholic, followed by years regretting how he had treated his family and forced them away. He spent his final days in a tiny unkempt trailer choosing to suffer.

There are those of us who approach death and are disastrously unprepared, then there are those that look to others who have passed this way before to shed some light on their own journey. The poem "Rocks" in the chapter Sticky Stuff is about learning from the struggles of others. Sometimes we choose to keep our burdens like martyrs and often we need help to let them go. It is moving towards a selfless soul when the rocks of burden or despair are laid down to aid another. The next part of the journey is to build these rocks into a bridge, not for you or even for a family member, but they might help the journey of a stranger.

"Angst" is a poem that is perhaps the one that resonates closely with my own feelings. I am exceptionally lucky to have both my parents and even my grandparents on my mother's side and though the poem speaks of a losing a mother, it really speaks to any loss and having difficulty expressing sadness. I suppose for me this poem is really about dealing with my sticky stuff, and working through those emotions that can be so painful. Perhaps it is my stiff upper lip, or my strong resolve, but there comes a time when you need to feel your emotions and cry. It is not until these painful feelings that are packed tightly in our cupboards see the light of day that we can begin our healing process.

There are several poems about helping loved ones on their journeys, "It's My Turn" is about the struggle of the patient losing independence and the family members wanting to help with the care. Of course the more help needed often signifies increased illness and moving closer to death. It is often hard to accept help, which in reality is accepting the truth of the situation. However family members often feel helpless, they want to give, as in this poem when a daughter wishes to return the care to her mum that she received as a child.

"I Am Here", was written for the visitors who come to see the sick and dying. They have the visitor watch that does not read the signs that it is time to leave. As you progress on your journey towards death it is common to want your world closer to you. Strange as it may seem you no longer care if the Red Sox win or lose, and you don't have the energy for light conversation with a dear old friend. These visitors can be seen at the bedside for hours, with the patient trying desperately to keep awake and entertain. They feel there is a certain visitor time frame to adhere to, to make the visit count. Then there are those at the other end of the spectrum who don't visit, they are afraid of what to say, or not to say. For all of them, "I Am Here" gives advice in sitting quietly and offering your comforting presence at the bedside of a dying friend.

Of course there are several poems about hospice itself. Hospice in the United States cares for people who have a life limiting illness and a prognosis of six months or less. Signing up for hospice for some can be too tough a reality. Who would not want to accept physical, emotional, or spiritual help in the dying process? There are many including doctors who decline the help of the midwife of death. "Hospice Nurse" is about how hospice does not change death, perhaps the journey to it, but not the end result. Recent research actually shows people who sign up for hospice live longer than those that do not and of course are usually more comfortable as well.

"Pain" is a poem that I almost kept in my cupboard. Not because it is my sticky stuff, but because it seems awkward to me. However my wonderful poetry support group felt that pain itself was an awkward subject that is difficult and complicated. The poem about pain speaks to how patients often have to learn and understand the medical terminology of pain medication even before they can get assistance. The world of pain medication is complicated enough from a nursing perspective never mind the elderly patient who desperately wants relief.

There are two poems that resonate with the psychosocial side of dying. "Cloak" in particular is a garment I have often seen worn by patients who feel so personally responsible for their inability to conquer their illness and postpone death. Of course when their chemotherapy no longer shrinks a tumor there can be a feeling of personal responsibility in losing the fight, but this was a race they could not win, and need to feel brave about fighting not losing.

Finally there are two poems that speak to death and animals. I have always loved animals and this poem is about my work at a local horse rescue farm. Some horses were only there for a short time, all enjoyed a little bit of heaven before their final ride. "Trail to Heaven" is about that journey.

"Understanding" is the remarkable story of a cat that made such a difference in a man's life. He was admitted to Hospice and wanted a cat. So the social worker went to the animal rescue league and found Sabrina. Immediately Sabrina spent her days beside her companion and did not move even after he had died. It was as though she knew her role in the house, and even after his death she now sits proudly next to his wife to comfort her. How wonderful an experience can be even without words and just purrs.

Angst

When the dark clouds closed in,
and she could not take another breath
through the pressure in her chest -
when the lump in her throat filled up
like a clump of dead leaves in a storm drain -
and when the words 'I'm fine'
got caught like a rabbit
on a barbed wire fence,
she finally cried.

She cried the loss of her mother,
her friend, her duty, her relationship.
She sobbed the past and the future,
her voice, her smell;
and the sobs and the cries
soothed like gentle healing ointment
on an open wound,
and slowly she began to heal.

It's My Turn

Mum, remember when you
took me in your arms
and melted away my pains
with your soothing voice.

Remember when you
gently bathed my body,
rubbing lotion into my skin.

Remember when I walked,
and you walked beside me
to catch me if I stumbled.

Remember when you stayed
beside me and told me
not to be afraid.

Now mum,
it's my turn.
Let me do
the same for you.

I Am Here

I am here
to be with you
in the silence of the day;
breathe your same air
and let the moment last
as long as it may.

I am here for you -
to listen to your stories,
turn them into memories,
like the earth turning under the plough.

I am giving,
not my voice,
but my presence.

I Am Not Ready

Through a semi-conscious haze,
death waits for me,
wearing the clothes of familiarity
of those that have gone before.

Daily I eat less,
yet dine heavily on memories of my life -
the bitterness of regret interspersed
with sweet morsels of reminiscent pleasure.

The reality of my situation
is the sharp pain in my soul,
intensifying with the momentum
I am gathering towards the Promised Land.

I am told to let go,
to have faith I will not fall
but rise up towards the heavens,
and I reply, "I am not ready.
I am too young to die."

Hospice Nurse

I am your angel and your darkness.

I come to comfort and soothe your journey.

I am the representation of your truth,

and while taking your blood pressure,

you ask nervously,

"What can I expect?"

Like an avalanche down a mountain,

the rumbling begins.

Your world will turn and twist,

eventually quieting to peace.

I cannot change its path,

but I will do my best to be here with you.

Stolen

I look in the mirror
and I am no longer there.
My self has been stolen
day by day.

The soft curves of my womanliness are missing,
replaced by a protruding frame
that looks back at me with awkward frailty.

The brightness in my eyes has gone,
morphed into a dull flicker
that winks knowingly at my pending fate.

Dignity has been misplaced,
and replaced with resignation.
My femininity flaps in the gale
of the tornado I am imprisoned in.

My cancer is a cruel thief
who steals me,
not all at once,
but piece by piece;
taking away what is not his to take
and forcing me to gaze into my death.

Oh Gentle Man

Oh gentle man who quietly came into my life
and melded in so effortlessly,
I felt I had always known you.

What special gifts you shared with me;
I shall forever be warmed by your smile.

How changed I am for having known you,
and would not trade a moment of your presence,
or the memories that I have saved.

I have walked my path through life,
and we have walked side by side
for just one moment,
and we have laughed and cried,
and I have felt honored to be your friend.
Oh gentle man, I will miss you.

In memory of my friend and colleague Peter

Seasons of Cancer

Spring came with new growth,
unnoticed and overlooked
yet unknowingly fed by her.

Undetectable and sly,
her cancer grew,
spreading itself
through her.

The summer was hot and dry
as she baked beneath her radiation treatments
and became parched with the side effects of her drugs.

Through autumn her hair began to fall
like the discarded leaves from the trees
outside her bedroom window.

It is winter;
her scans show
barren fields
empty of the growth
she did not plant.

She is seasoned now,
and is prepared for spring
and many springs to come.

Pain

Pain struck down on me
like lightning from an angry sky.
Screaming out
in a language I did not understand, I did not speak -

Visceral !
Sciatic !
Neuropathic !

My doctor and my nurse shout back in tongue.

Narcotic !
Adjunctive !
Q4hours !
QAC !
Round the clock !

In fear of what is to come,
I join the chant -

Pre-medicate !

Sublingual !

Analgesic !

Now !!

Hope

Hope is not
the CAT scans
or blood transfusions.

Hope lies deep
within the soul
of every one of us.

Sometimes we find it
in the quiet reflection of being alone,
sometimes holding tight to a friend with sobs of realization.

Hope is not the chemo or the radiation.
It is the spirit that helps us start another day.

It is not the lab values or the blood test results.
It is the power of family and friends to support and nurture.

It is not the ups and downs,
but the riding of the storm
and the vision of blue skies and calmer water ahead.

Thirsty

How thirsty do you have to be
before you will drink?

How many nails will dig deep
into the wood of your coffin
before you realize you are still alive?

Stand still a moment
and let yourself be loved.

Understanding

She understood
without words or gestures,
when others wanted to look away.

She understood the need for
sleep,
company,
reassurance,
touch,
space.

She stayed there
until the end,
when the undertaker lifted her from his side.

Her name is Sabrina,
the cat.

How Much Longer

How much longer do you wait?
...and feel guilty for waiting
and wishing a death to come.

Pleading for death,
then in the same breath,
pleading for life -
just one more day
or hour, or minute -
a life for a life,
a pile of regrets for a promise,
an end to this moment
that feels like eternity.

In Hospice

In hospice I do not see death,
I see love.

I have seen love
caught behind anger,
hidden in shame,
spread on toast.

I have seen love
dropped in one tear,
seasoned into soup,
lotioned into skin.

I have seen love
without words,
between yells,
within whispers -

and I have been honored
to have been witness
to so much.

The Trail to Heaven

Rest awhile and let the stories of your life soften
amidst the comfort of a full belly.
Let us soothe your wounds
that speak to us from deep inside your soul.

We are grateful that you chose
the safety of our love and care
to be your last memory before your hooves
touch the trails of Heaven.

The memory of your strength and spirit
will forever course through our veins,
and from Heaven you will let others know
of this place where paradise is found.

Lonely

Family and friends surround me
and yet I feel lonely -

lonely because I am the only one
who can make this journey;

lonely because they can empathize with me
but they do not feel the nerves that inform me every day
that my cancer is still a growing part of me,

and they do not feel the nausea that I push down
to make room for my food.

They have imagination
to understand my journey.

I have reality
knocking on my door,
like the thunderstorm
that starts in the distance
and becomes louder with every clap.

Judgment Day

Previously stretching far behind,
his past now crowds around him,
snapping at his heels,
and whispering long forgotten memories
into his mind.

Arguments that lay deep for many years,
pull like lobster traps
tethered from the bottom of the ocean.

Regrets of decisions
simmer to the surface,
ready for the boil.

And rolling around,
and back and forth,
are the doubts
that forgiveness will be served
on Judgment Day.

One Choice

I am standing still
and absorbing one more memory.

Each single ray of sunshine tingles on my face
and reminds me of the simplicity of life
that I am living
while I am dying.

Initially confused,
now I understand the voice of my cancer,
speaking directly to my soul.

The choice is not the end,
but living to the end.

Cloak

Lift up the cloak
that hides your shame
for not having fought hard enough.

Open yourself bare to me,
so I can share
the wounds of disappointment,
that you failed your treatment,
that there is nothing else to do.

Let me step closer
and help erase doubt,
for you have only shown strength
and you are more whole now then you ever were.

Life

There is one thing that working with death everyday makes us do, and that is appreciate life. It is not easy, there are many things that can distract you from making the most of each day, but if it is a conscious effort then there will be success.

I remember having a conversation with my sister and how relieved she was to read some of my poetry that was on topics other than death. She remarked that not everyone lives in a world that faces death everyday, and she reminded me of how "normal" it felt to me. So the poems in this chapter are dedicated to my sister who helps me to appreciate what a unique experience it is to face the ultimate challenge on a daily basis.

I have looked after many patients who had worked hard all their lives and were looking forward to their retirement only to get diagnosed with a life limiting illness and sign up for the support of hospice. They urged me not to put off what was really important to me and ultimately not to look back and wish something had been different in my life. So I quit my job, rented out my house and with my partner, my dad and my two pugs drove 15,000 miles in 3 months to see the United States of

America from campsites and a pop up trailer tent. Recently becoming an American citizen had fueled my desire to see the country that I had pledged allegiance to. What a wonderful place we saw, and there is not a day that goes by that some memory from that summer doesn't add a smile to my face.

My trans-America trip encouraged my passion for travel and so, not surprisingly, inspired many poems and consequently many are of traveling in the county of my birth, England. One of my favorite travel poems is called "England", which makes me wonder if I should start to get a little more creative with my titles. I came to Massachusetts, USA in 1989 to work in a summer camp as a nurse. My friend was camp nurse on the boy's camp and I was on the girl's camp. My brother came too and we had an amazing summer as I am sure does anyone who spends a summer on Cape Cod. I returned the following year to work in Boston and have been in the US for the remaining 16 years. I never thought when I came at 21 that I would spend the rest of my life in America, and sometimes I wonder where I will be in the coming years, but it's funny how one year melds into the next. Despite being an American citizen, loving my life here, my roots will always be in England and that will always be my ultimate home. I had the most idyllic childhood, growing up in a small village in the north called Stillington, and so of course there is a poem about my village.

There has been a lot of travel for me in the last six months with my new job and so too much inspiration for more travel poems. "Beware Arizona" was written while driving from Phoenix to Safford and witnessing spectacular breath-taking scenery. I stopped at an archaeological site along the way to take some pictures for my mum and in my excitement I sat on a cactus and shortly after wrote the poem.

For those who know me and my bubbly love of life there are a few whimsical poems such as the one called "Alien in my Soup"; the title came to me first and then the poetry second. I love aliens and anything science fiction, and we made sure on our cross county trip that we stopped at Roswell, New Mexico and learned all we could about area 51.

'Winter" is a poem that will need explaining for my international readers. There is a saying in New England from years ago that you are not allowed to wear white after Labor Day, which is the bank holiday that falls at the beginning of September. The poem "Winter" is a play on words from Old Man Winter talking about there being plenty of white in New England, and of course meaning that we would be facing a harsh winter with plenty of snow.

My most recent poems are about my new relationship and that wonderful place of falling in love.

So here you are, Annabel: my poems about life…

My Music

My music
wells from deep inside of me,
speaking from the soul
of fulfilling promises
laid at birth -

to open up
and let breathe
a long-awaited
celebration of self and life,
of purpose and passion;

to free the seeds
that lay within
and plant with pen and paper;

to be all that I can
and for others to share
and grow in turn.

Sisters...

A comforting connection,
a history from the beginning;

laughing,
smiling,
sharing,

a depth of understanding
from a place of knowing -

Friends...

Sisters.

English Village Stillington

Sleeping village,
waking up from winter's grasp;
with daffodil yellow floors
making way for pink shades of blossom,
hanging like curtains
under a pale blue sky -
attracting tourists from cityscapes
to dabble in the country air.

Alien in My Soup

It started in the morning
like an ordinary day.
I was driving down the highway,
and stopped along the way.

I was feeling kind of peckish,
so headed for a bite.
I got a bowl of soup
and also quite a fright.

For sitting on a crouton
and wishing me good day,
was a tiny little alien,
who chirped, then flew away.

What Does Vacation Look Like?

Nothing to do
but watch and wait.
Nothing to choose
but which trail to take.
Sitting and wondering
about what is in store;
Sampling life
on a foreign shore.

Exmoor Ponies

As rugged as the earth
beneath their hooves,
mares unkempt from wind tousled days,
spirit of freedom,
glinting amid a chestnut gaze.

Seeing Arizona

Arriving in Arizona
takes vision adjustment -
from the New Hampshire forests
to the red rock mountains and valley floors.
Nearsighted vision is perfect for the woods and trees
but at first could be disorientating,
with the vast expanse and seemingly endless roads.

The personality of the mountains changes throughout the day,
the dark cover of night receding
to expose colors of earth in rich red rusts.
As the sun moves the shadows throughout the day,
she changes the shades
witnessed by the mountain pass traveler.

There could be an addiction here,
as I breathe in the deep peace of astonishing vistas.
Could I trade New Hampshire woods
for Arizona desert?
The taste was tempting
but at present I will keep the vision
in my minds eye.

Feather

Like a feather,
taken up on the wind,
your love swept me up
into your arms.

I find myself falling,
for your gentleness,
for your kindness,
and when our eyes meet
amidst a close embrace,
I feel a need to pull you tight
and move closer still.

Blue Bonnets of Texas

How soothing to the eyes;
seas of blue
in wave on wave,
the Blue Bonnets of Texas.

Growing singularly and randomly,
yet together.

Oceans of delight
lapping around my feet
as I paddle amongst them.

Intrigued by their delicate nature,
I find myself sweetened by the simple pleasure
of blue bonnet pastures
captured in my mind.

Sunlight Fairies

It was on a magical twilight stroll
in a wood I had traveled many times before,
as the sunlight dipped low in the heavens,
and streamed through the leaves.

I saw their fairy wings soaking up the sunlight
all around me,
and I was encircled by a field of yellow.

Dancing Fairies

As the early morning air
filled the woods around me,
at first I heard their laughter
and then I saw them –
fairies everywhere,
twirling and swirling around and around.

They told me how important it was
to twirl and swirl
and I promised them I would never forget.

Today I Shall Visit Charlotte

Today I shall visit Charlotte.
I hear she is warm
and bathed in shining sun.
She has a background
laced and overflowing with history
of American birth
and civil war.

She speaks with a southern tongue
which may confuse an English girl -
but nothing that some winter sun
in North Carolina cannot soothe.

Sweet Dreams

The chipmunk comes to me in my dream,
I can even smell
the musky odor of its presence.

It calls to me
in sharp shrill blasts,
with an intensity that
flips my switch from sleep to wake,
and brings me to the instant realization,
that my cat is chasing the chipmunk
under my bed.

Connection

Looking for love,
that connects me like the last piece
of a puzzle.

Searching for an answer,
when the question
is still fluid in my mind.

Finding it in you,
who stood beside me
all along.

England

Green and pleasant land,
built of brick and slate roofs;
roots of blood and family ties,
holding on through
distance of lands and oceans,
inside every cell of me -
as part of me
as bone and brain.

New Job

I fit in my new job
like a baggy jacket -
it has great potential
but I have a long way to go.

Even the material feels alien against my skin
and I am eyed wonderingly in my uncomfortable attire.

Then as the threads of my first day pull tight,
I am warmed by a realization:
to make this jacket work,
I just have to have new shoes.

Beware the Arizona Desert

Beware the Arizona desert,
not for the rattlesnake -
it is still hibernating 'til February;

not for the scorpion -
there were none to be seen;

definitely not for dehydration -
we have ten inches of snow
melting into the ground;

but for the cactus,
whose needles will quickly
bite into your buttocks
as you squat to have your photo taken.

And then begins the operation of extraction
and the feelings all day
that perhaps some spines were left behind.

Winter

The crescendo of autumn colors
rustling to the ground
does not drown the laughter of
winter whispering in my ear,

"No white after Labor Day -
        Ha ha!
  There'll be plenty of white
     this year, my dear."

March on Cape Cod

There is anticipation in the dunes,
waiting for the sun to warm the days
and bring back the crowds of summer.

Presently the ocean spends its time
sweeping the beach for memories,
of summer fun,
laughter,
melting ice-creams,
and first love.

Footprints left in the sand have long been
washed back into the ocean.

The boardwalks are silent from the chatter of
eager tourists feet,
and the beach patiently waits.

Airport

Shadows stretch across the tarmac,
almost at the climax of their show,
before dusk will take them back
into the blackness of the night ahead -

Metal birds perched with arms outstretched,
in a feeding frenzy for their journey.

All nations together
like a mixed fruit salad,
listening to the beckoning of their destinations,
waiting for the gate to open
and the race to begin.

Sleep Tight

Sleep tight
while I am away,
for tonight I will
visit you in your dreams.

Kissing you gently
on your forehead,
to melt the furrows
in your brow.

Holding you close,
infusing a calming antidote to the
troubles in your day,
and sending you deeper
into sleep,
while I lay by your side.

My Medicine

I take medicine in a daily dose
to soothe a jam-packed mind;
I don't take a prescription,
rather anything I can find.

Sometimes it's a spoon of sunshine
streaking through the clouds;
sometimes it's my favorite song
sung raucously out loud.

Each day before breakfast
I drink a cup of smiles;
it keeps the ticker ticking
for endless miles on miles.

I keep some for emergencies
when my energy is low;
I'll take a spoon of silly jokes
and watch my power grow.

Love Grows

When love flows like a cascading waterfall

and souls swirl together,

in that magical place

where love grows,

there is no pace

of fast or slow.

There is just love

between two people,

who are meant to be together.

Sticky Stuff

This is the chapter that contains the sticky stuff. The sticky stuff are the poems about those things in life that teach us lessons and make us stronger. The sticky stuff is also the stuff that we want to avoid, but often get stuck in anyway, and for me there are plenty of sticky poems here that I almost didn't include in this book. However my fabulous poetry group encouraged me not to leave these poems in the darkness of my cupboard.

As I have added more years to my nursing belt I have become convinced that the only good thing about a terminal illness is that it gives you a chance to say the things you need to say and do the things you need to do, as opposed to an accident where death is sudden and unexpected. Of course we should be living each day by saying and doing those things, but most of us leave at least a small helping for that final approach, hoping we still have time. The poem that developed from my witness to many people who could not say the things they needed to, is called "Communication". It was inspired by the anger that explodes from the situations that people are trying to deal with. Often the arguments or family rifts are from petty squabbles long forgotten, however the bitterness of betrayal and the struggle not to lose keep the anger stoked. Some families when facing death come together and take this opportunity to heal, and hospice takes time to give people the tools to help them. I have cared for many parents who linger on their deathbed, terribly concerned about what will happen to the family after they die. They have been the peacemaker through the previous years and fear that when they die all threads of family will disintegrate. This poem is not just about the deathbed though but anytime there is an angry situation or disagreement. What is truly needed is not fuel for the fire, but for someone to say, "I am sorry", to start the healing process and begin a direction of moving forward.

Most of the poems in this chapter do not need my explanation, though I think the poetic reader may be interested in my reasons for writing them and perhaps compare the stickiness factor. There are two poems that come from a particular hospice experience called "Heal" and "Egg". Our Hospice Chaplain has been a mentor to me in my spiritual growth and one day in particular has strong memories for me. It was Spring/Easter time at work and she had worked hard the day before coloring hard boiled eggs, and decorating each egg with one word written in glue glitter pen. The eggs where all laid in the basket with their words concealed and as we began our meeting she passed the basket around. We each took an egg, and were to spend the next few minutes contemplating the word we had received from our eggs. Of twenty eggs laid in the basket, amidst words like fun, laugh and play, was a single word meant for me: "heal". I knew the word was meant for me. I had been feeling emotionally worn out and knew I needed to take some time for myself. The word was as simple as it could be, in a child's glitter glue pen, however I had been afraid to let down my strong armor and spend time with the softer side of my nature. The second poem "Egg" speaks to that fear.

No sticky chapter would be complete without poems about relationships and in the past year I have been delving into rather a lot of relationship stickies. Earlier this year I ended a relationship of seventeen years, and spent time in the following months to redefine myself. I am wondering though if some of my redefinition had more to do with turning forty but either way, it's all sticky. I also found love in a place I didn't expect and of course wrote poems about that which you will find in the Life chapter.

My poems continue to help me process, to try to understand the feelings and emotions that seem so confusing and mixed up in the turmoil of the day. So here's to letting the sticky stuff out of the cupboard. Enjoy.

Let Me

Let me repair
the threads of our lives
that got so tangled.

Let me soothe
the wounds
that cut so deep into your soul.

Give me a chance
to say the words
that should have been said so long ago.

Let me be
what I should have been,
do what I didn't do.

I am here now
to say I love you.

Rocks

Oh how selfish to keep the weight of despair,
like heavy rocks,
loaded down inside a bag
upon your back.

Use them instead
to build a bridge,
to help the next weary traveler
that comes this way.

Heal

Oh what excitement,
Easter is here,
and like children,
we circle around the basket
and wait for our colored egg.

On each egg is
one word,
a message to the soul.
Amidst words of "dance", "sing" and "fun",
I have picked the word "heal",
but I don't want to heal.

I have heard this word before
from the depths of my being,
but I haven't listened -
I don't want to listen now.

However, it comes to me in not just two,
but three dimensions,
written in glitter glue pen,
calling out to me -
to heal.

Sipping Bitterness

Will the feeling that
I must move in this direction
lessen the pain of memories,
being taken from their frames
and turned inside out?

Could the knowledge of this truth,
running like jolts of electricity
through my body,
numb the sadness in my heart?

Will it hurt less
if I feel it all at once
or drag it out,
sipping on this bitterness daily?

Becoming

Her body changed
and her skin grew tighter,
almost feeling as if the air was taken away
and she could no longer live
beneath the falseness.

She could not tell
if the metamorphosis was new,
or if her mind had shielded her
from what was now
racing through every cell
within her soul -

a voice that would not be silenced,
a tempting desire to fulfill,
a softness between souls,
of sensual breaths
panting with passion -
unleashed from knowing
that this felt so right,
and there was no other direction,
to go.

Your Betrayal

Your betrayal
settled into a spear,
that penetrates deep into my
spirit and my soul,
and straight through any semblance
of remaining sanity.

I am surprised you cannot see
the blood from my wounds,
soaking into my shirt.

The love we shared
now pools and coagulates between us,
separating forever,
the connection together.

So I use this energy of disbelief,
and aching wounds to gain strength,
for my journey ahead.

The Dance

What has been forbidden fruit
now sits ripened before me,
blond hair and hazel eyes
calling to my senses,
opening the flood gates,
and swirling through my mind.

With first date confusion,
thoughts of gentle caressing
and exchanging breaths
in an intimate embrace,
flicker amidst the question:
Will I remember the dance?

Stitches

We have been entwining our lives

for seventeen years,

and now I must

pick apart by hand,

the stitches that kept us together.

Letting them unravel,

into what ever they may come.

Sadness

If the sadness in my heart is ignored,
Will I feel it less?

If I let it creep up
and spill out into my tears,
Will it soothe my pain?

Communication

A miscommunication
tangled and flared up,
as angry teeth
on raw tattered flesh -

so hard to bow down
and offer up,
like a warrior without sword or shield -
to say "I'm sorry".

Egg

My skin that I have worked
so hard to be thick and protective,
surprises me at its brittleness;
like the egg I hold in my hand,
whose shell appears complete,
but is so easy to smash and break
into a thousand million pieces -
and I fear if I break,
how difficult it would be
to place those pieces
where they were,
and to feel whole again.

Moving Forward

It isn't so much about putting one step in front of the other
but making sure you are facing in the right direction.
Finding time to rest,
adding nourishment and energy to continue.

It isn't how long the journey takes
but that you are aware of the journey
and the need to move forward.

It is getting up again when you fall,
catching yourself when you falter,
holding on to support
even if you are only standing still.

It is not the perpetual forward motion
but turning towards the sun,
letting the spirit rise -
honoring the uniqueness of your soul,
your past journey
and your desire to move forward.

Change

My life settles around me,
like flour on a bakers table,
continually reconfiguring with even the slightest breeze;
and as a wave of change
creeps up on me like nausea,
I hold on tighter to the unraveling rope of my stability.

Gingerly I move into the realization
that change is as much a part of me and my world
as the air I breathe;
and like the currents in the ocean,
I can move with them,
or against them.

Writing Your Own Poems

This is the chapter that will inspire you to write and create your own poems, by using step by step instructions.

Rules:

There are no rules. These are your poems and your inspiration. You can use them for your own personal growth and processing, share them with your family, friends and colleagues or you can publish them and become rich and famous.

Getting Started:

A little bit of preparation will help. So having a paper and pen handy or a tape recorder will mean you can capture your inspiration straight away.

When and Where:

Think about when you may have a few minutes for inspiration. Is it at bedtime before you go to sleep or sitting in the car while you wait for the kids to get out of school? You don't need a lot of time and sometimes my greatest inspiration can occur while I am sitting at a light or stuck in traffic.

Let's write a poem:

Start by thinking of a question and what your answers are. Try these questions and write in your answers.

❯ What kind of things do you do to help other people?

❯ Why are they important?

❯ How does it make you feel?

Your poem is going to have:

> Subject – What is it about?
>
> Beginning – opening
>
> Middle – the middle
>
> End – wrapping up

Think about adding some phrases with the word "**like**", it helps you describe something and paint the picture for your audience.

For example in the poem **Angst** using the word "**like**" really helps to show how she is feeling.

> "When the dark clouds closed in,
>
> and she could not take another breath
>
> through the pressure in her chest -
>
> when the lump in her throat filled up
>
> **like** a clump of dead leaves in a storm drain -
>
> and when the words 'I'm fine'
>
> got caught **like** a rabbit
>
> on a barbed wire fence,"

Let's try writing a poem by filling in the blanks:

The _____ lady

Sat _____

And _____

Like _____

Her _____ arrived _____

And _____

The lady _____

Filled in it might look something like this:

The *anxious* **lady**

Sat *with hands wound up in knotted bedclothes*

And *waited for the doorbell*

Like *the ringer on the stove signaling she was done.*

Her *daughter* **arrived** *and began to rub lotion into her hands soothing the rough skin*

And *she observed that the lotion also soothed the sharp edges of her worries. As the visit came to a close,*

The lady *wondered if perhaps next time her daughter could rub her back as she felt the sharp edges of worry there too.*

Now try this one:

The_____caregiver_____

into the kitchen and_____

like_____

The patient _____

And when the caregiver returned_____

Like_____

She_____

It might end up something like this:

The *weary* **caregiver** *stepped into the kitchen and stood* **like** *a dear in headlights*

The patient *curled up in bed and wrapped beneath crocheted Afghans did not even have enough energy for thoughts of the past or the future, only of the present moment*

And when the caregiver returned *plates laden*

Like *a Thanksgiving banquet she realized it was not the food that made Thanksgiving but rather the giving of thanks*

She *put down the plates, reached out, took her husband's hand and quietly whispered into his ear "Thanks for everything my dear"*

Your poems:

Remember your poems don't have to rhyme, win awards or solve answers. They are your poems, be confident that you are capable and that you owe it to yourself to write. Make time to do what is important for you and your own wellbeing.

Remember that you are the only one that will stand at the end of your life and look back. Don't stand there and wish you had been a poet!

Deepest appreciation and many thanks to my family and friends for all their support.

And special thanks to:

Andrew and Lev for their title inspiration,

My poetry group who gave me the courage to publish even my stickiest poems,

Mike for expanding my poetry horizons,

Healing Environments for their hospitality of my poetry group,

and Dede for seventeen years of support and inspiration.